WHY DO BONES BREAK?

✦ and other questions about movement ✦

Angela Royston

www.heinemann.co.uk/library

Visit our website to find out more information about **Heinemann Library** books.

To order:

 Phone 44 (0) 1865 888066

 Send a fax to 44 (0) 1865 314091

 Visit the Heinemann Bookshop at www.heinemann.co.uk/library to browse our catalogue and order online.

First published in Great Britain by Heinemann Library, Halley Court, Jordan Hill, Oxford OX2 8EJ, a division of Reed Educational and Professional Publishing Ltd. Heinemann is a registered trademark of Reed Educational & Professional Publishing Limited.

OXFORD MELBOURNE AUCKLAND JOHANNESBURG BLANTYRE
GABORONE IBADAN PORTSMOUTH NH (USA) CHICAGO

Designed by Joanna Sapwell and StoryBooks
Illustrations by Nick Hawken
Originated by Ambassador Litho Ltd
Printed in China by South China Printing Company

ISBN 0 431 11075 1
06 05 04 03 02
10 9 8 7 6 5 4 3 2 1

British Library Cataloguing in Publication Data
Royston, Angela
Why do bones break?.– (Body matters)
1. Bones – Juvenile literature 2. Fractures – Juvenile literature
I.Title
612.7'5

Acknowledgements
The Publishers would like to thank the following for permission to reproduce photographs:
Corbis: 14, 15; David Walker: 27; Gareth Boden: 17, 20, 21, 23, 24, 28; Powerstock/Zefa: 10, 11, 12; Science Photo Library: 7, 8, 18, 19, 26.

Cover photograph reproduced with permission of Powerstock/Zefa.

Our thanks to Anne Long for her help in the preparation of this book.

Every effort has been made to contact copyright holders of any material reproduced in this book. Any omissions will be rectified in subsequent printings if notice is given to the Publisher.

CONTENTS

Words printed in **bold letters like these** are explained in the Glossary.

WHAT DO BONES DO?

Bones are the frame that supports your body and gives it its shape. Without bones you would be as floppy as a lump of jelly. Bones also protect important parts of your body, such as your heart.

The skeleton

Each bone is hard and strong. You can feel hard bone below most of your soft flesh. Together the bones make up your **skeleton** and it gives you your basic shape. Animals, such as horses, elephants and mice, are different sizes and shapes to humans because their skeletons are different sizes and shapes.

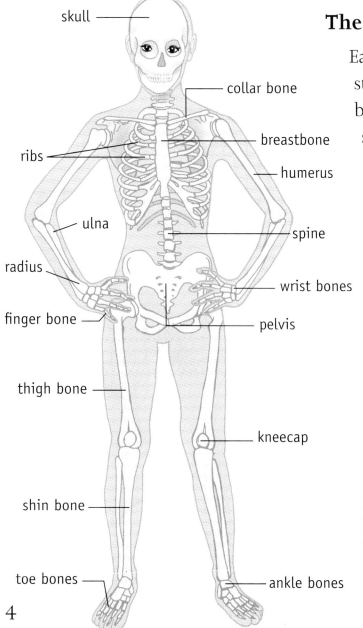

skull

collar bone

breastbone

humerus

ribs

ulna

spine

radius

wrist bones

finger bone

pelvis

thigh bone

kneecap

shin bone

toe bones

ankle bones

Your skeleton is made up of all the bones in your body.

4

Number of bones

You have many bones in your body. Babies have more than 350 bones when they are born but, as they grow, some of the bones join together. For example, babies have nine small bones at the bottom of their spine. By the time they are adult, these will have joined together to make just two bones. Adults have about 206 bones. About half of all adult bones are in the hands and feet. Each hand and foot has 26 different bones.

The smallest bones are in your ears. They help to pass sound through your ear. The smallest is the stirrup and it is no longer than a grain of rice.

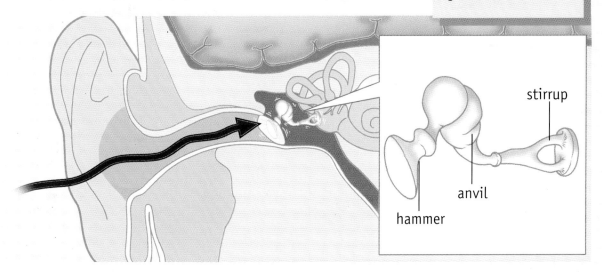

stirrup

anvil

hammer

WHAT IS THE LONGEST BONE IN THE BODY?

The thigh bone is the longest bone. It reaches from the hip to the knee and is about the same length as your spine. It makes up between a quarter and a third of your total height.

A suit of armour

Bones protect important parts of your body, such as your brain and **kidneys**. These parts of the body are **organs** and you cannot survive without them. Bones help to protect them from bangs, bumps and blows.

The skull

The skull is the hard bone that forms the shape of your head and face. It is made up of 22 different bones. Twenty-one of these are fused together so that they cannot move. There are holes in your skull for your eyes, ears, nostrils and mouth. The lower jaw is the only bone in the skull that can move.

The skull protects the brain, the eyes, ears and mouth. The only bone that can move is the lower jaw. You move it to chew and to talk.

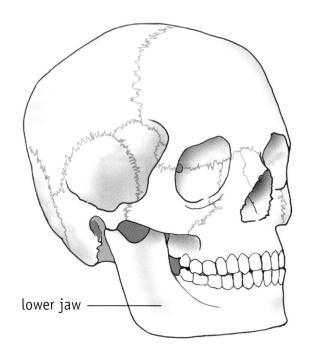

lower jaw

Ribs and breastbone

You have twelve ribs on each side of your body. One end of each rib is joined to the spine. It curves round your side and joins your breastbone. This forms a cage that protects your heart and lungs. The lowest two pairs of ribs are called floating ribs because they do not join the breastbone.

The pelvis

The pelvis is made up of several bones that protect your **intestines** and other soft organs. The biggest bones in the pelvis are the hip bones. When you sit down, most of your weight rests on the hip bones.

The spine

The spine (backbone) is made up of 26 separate **vertebrae**. Each one has a hole through the middle. **Nerves** from all over the body pass through the vertebrae and are protected by them. These nerves, called the spinal cord, carry messages between the brain and the rest of the body except the head.

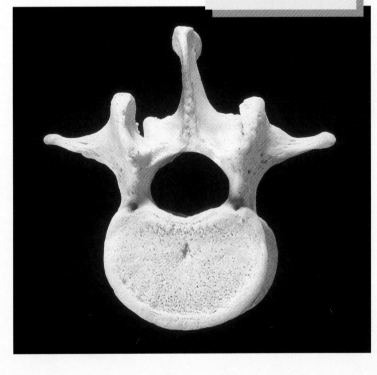

This single vertebra is one of the bones that make up the spine. The holes in the middle of the vertebrae form a hollow column that contains the spinal cord.

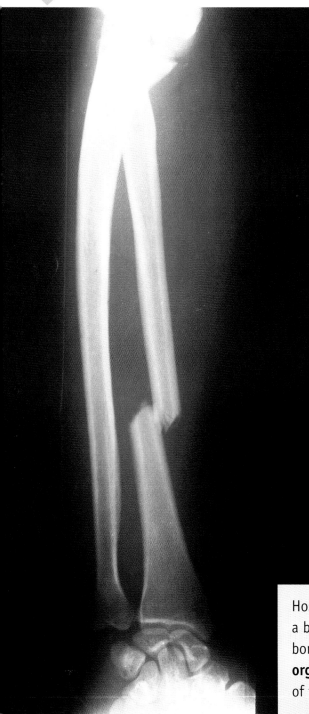

WHY DO BONES BREAK?

Bones break when they are snapped, crushed or hit very hard. If you fell off the climbing frame and landed awkwardly on your arm, one of the bones in your arm might crack or break. Bones break because they are hard and do not bend as rubber does.

What makes bones hard?

Bone is one of the hardest substances in your body. Only the enamel which coats the outside of your teeth is harder. Bones contain **minerals** and it is these that make them hard, especially the mineral calcium phosphate. Minerals make up nearly half the contents of bone. The rest is water and living substances such as blood **cells** and bone cells.

Hospitals use x-rays to check whether a bone is broken. An x-ray shows the bones but not the soft flesh or **organs**. This person has broken one of the bones in their lower arm.

Strong bones

Bones are not only hard – they are strong. The strongest bones are the long bones in your arms and legs. They are shaped like a cylinder, one of the strongest natural shapes. The hardest and strongest part of the bone is on the outside. It is called compact bone. Below the compact bone is softer, spongy bone. It is lighter than compact bone and, without it, your arms and legs would be very heavy. The spongy bone acts as a shock absorber, particularly at the ends of the long bones. If the end of the bone is banged, the spongy bone absorbs much of the shock.

BONE MARROW

The inside of a bone is hollow and filled with red or yellow bone **marrow**. Red bone marrow is the factory that makes new blood cells. Yellow bone marrow is mainly fat.

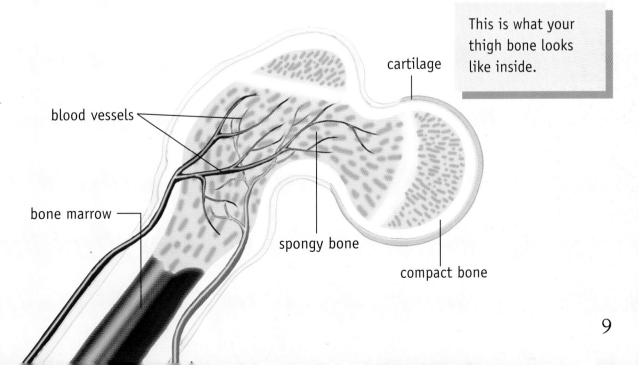

This is what your thigh bone looks like inside.

cartilage

blood vessels

bone marrow

spongy bone

compact bone

DO BONES BLEED?

Bones are made of living **cells**. Like all other living cells in the human body, they need blood to supply them with food and oxygen. The inside of a bone is criss-crossed with tiny tubes carrying blood. If the bone is cracked or broken, blood and bone **marrow** ooze into the break. You usually cannot see the blood because it is covered with flesh and skin.

Making sure the bone is straight

If you think you may have broken a bone, you should go to hospital to have it checked. A doctor has to make sure that the bone is straight before it begins to mend. If the broken bone is

This boy broke his arm when he fell off his bicycle. The cast protects the bone while it mends. The cast stops him from moving his elbow.

crooked it will mend like that. If a bone in your arm or leg is broken, the doctor will wrap a special bandage around it. When the wet bandage dries, it forms a hard cast. This protects the bone while it mends and makes sure that it stays straight.

Repairing a break

A broken or cracked bone mends itself. At first the area around the break may be very swollen. The swelling helps to protect the damaged bone. The crack is plugged with blood and marrow. Slowly new bone grows across the break. Most breaks heal in a month or two, but some may take up to a year. Old people's bones take longer to heal. When a child's bone has healed it will probably be as strong as it was before the break.

As a broken bone heals, new bone grows across the gap. Inside, the gap is filled with new bone marrow.

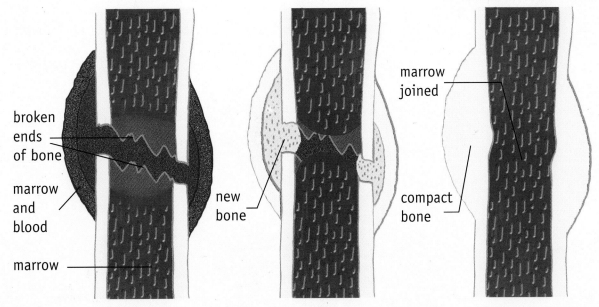

broken
ends
of bone

marrow
and
blood

marrow

new
bone

marrow
joined

compact
bone

HOW FAST DO BONES GROW?

Babies have short legs and arms and large heads compared with the rest of the body. As children grow, the long bones in their legs and arms gradually catch up.

Bones grow very slowly. They grow fastest in the first two years of life. By this time a child will have reached about half his or her adult height. It then takes another fourteen to sixteen years to grow as tall again. Bones do not grow at a constant rate. Children have growth spurts when they suddenly grow a few centimetres taller. Then their growth may slow down for a year or two. During **puberty**, children grow very quickly for a few years, but gradually slow down as they reach their adult height.

How bones grow

Bones develop from **cartilage**. Cartilage is the rubbery substance you can feel at the end of your nose. When a baby is born, its bones are mainly cartilage. This means that babies' bones are softer than children's and adult bones.

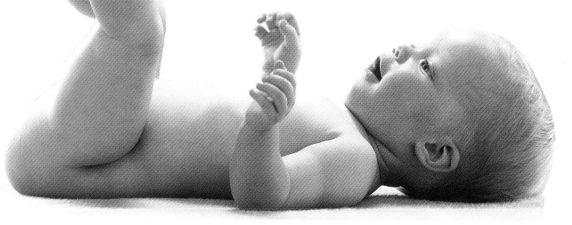

The cartilage slowly hardens into bone and new cartilage forms at the ends of the bones. Bone is harder than cartilage because it contains more calcium. Babies take in calcium from the milk they drink.

Cushioning the bones

Cartilage also grows at the end of the long bones in your arms and legs. Here it forms a cushion that protects the bones from shocks and jolts as you run and jump. The bones in your spine are also cushioned with a pad of cartilage to stop them rubbing together.

A long bone from an adult and from a child. The child's bone has more cartilage at the ends, which will slowly harden into bone.

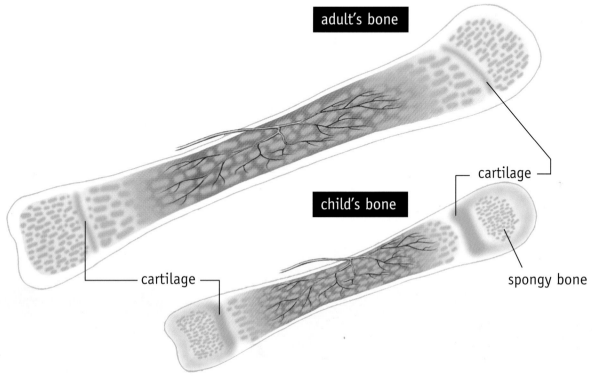

adult's bone

cartilage

child's bone

cartilage

spongy bone

WHY DO MY KNEES BEND BUT NOT TWIST?

Joints are where two or more bones meet. You can move your body only at your joints, and the shape of the joint decides how the bones move. The knee is the joint between the thigh bone and the shin. The shape of the knee joint allows you to bend your knee but not to twist it. Other joints allow different kinds of movement.

A ball and socket joint allows you to twist as well as bend.

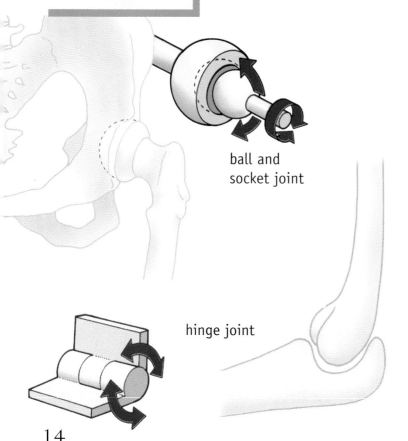

ball and socket joint

hinge joint

Knee joint

The joints at your knee and elbow are called hinge joints, because they work like the hinge of a door. Your knee allows you to bend your lower leg back and then to straighten it again, but you cannot bend it forward. Your knees have to be strong because they carry the weight of most of your body. A hinge joint is strongest when the bones are in a straight line and the joint is locked. If your knees could twist easily, they would constantly give way beneath you.

KINDS OF JOINTS

Hinge joints:	knee, elbow, fingers, toes
Ball and socket:	hip, shoulder
Pivot:	neck
Sliding:	wrist, ankle
Saddle:	thumb

Shoulder and hip

The hip and the shoulder are both ball and socket joints. In a ball and socket joint the rounded end of a long bone fits into a deep cup or socket. It allows you to move your arm around at the shoulder in a circle in any direction. Similarly you can circle your upper leg in your hip.

This girl is using the ball and socket joints in her hip and shoulders to move her leg and upper arm.

Neck joint

The joint in your neck has to be strong to hold up your head. It is called a pivot joint because it has a pin that fits into a hole through a **vertebra**. The pin turns, or pivots, in the vertebra so that you can both turn your head and nod it up and down.

Wrist, ankle and thumb joints

There are many small bones in your wrists and ankles. They fit together in such a way that you can move your hands and feet from side to side as well as up and down. This type of joint allows the bones to slide against each other. You have much more movement in your thumb than you do in each of your fingers. Your fingers can curl to grip, but your thumb can move all around.

> The neck is a pivot joint, the thumb is a saddle joint and the wrist and ankle are sliding joints.

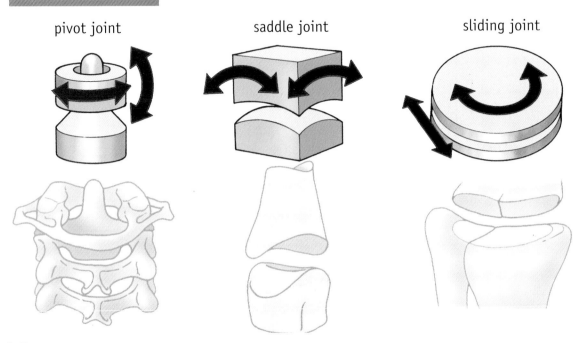

pivot joint   saddle joint   sliding joint

Most important of all, your thumb can touch each of your finger tips. This allows you to hold and move a pen, knife and fork and other instruments.

Spine

The bones in your spine are called **vertebrae**. They fit together to make a strong column that supports your head but allows you to twist around. If you stand still you can twist your spine and neck together to see behind you. Almost all the other bones in the **skeleton** are either attached directly to the spine or are attached to it through other bones.

Skull

Apart from your lower jawbone, the bones in your head cannot move. They are joined together by fixed joints.

The bones in your back fit together to allow you to bend forwards, backwards and from side to side. They also allow you to twist.

WHY DO MY KNUCKLES CRACK?

No one knows for sure why your **knuckle** sometimes cracks when you pull your finger straight. It may be that a bubble of gas forms in the liquid inside the joint and it cracks as it bursts. Or it may be that the joint has formed a seal, like that made on a jar of jam in the factory. When you open the jar for the first time, the seal pops.

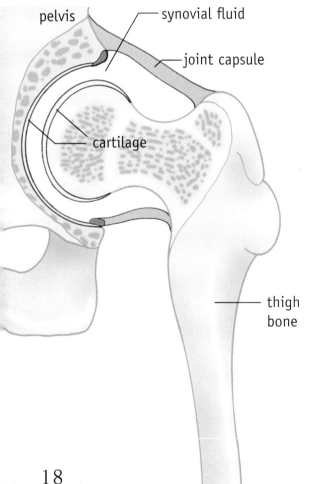

pelvis — synovial fluid

joint capsule

cartilage

thigh bone

Inside a joint

A joint has to allow the bones to move smoothly. If the bones rubbed against each other when they moved, it would be very painful and the bones would soon wear out. The ends of the bones are cushioned by **cartilage** which is soft and slippery and allows the bones to move comfortably. Many joints are also oiled by a liquid called synovial fluid.

Cartilage and synovial fluid allow the joint to move smoothly. The capsule keeps the liquid inside the joint.

Ligaments

A joint has to be strong so that it only moves when you want it to and it does not move too far. Ligaments are tough bands of gristle that join the bones across a joint. They are strong but slightly stretchy. They hold the bones together and stop them from slipping out of the joint.

Twists and sprains

Ligaments can become damaged if they are stretched too far. If you twist your ankle, for instance, you may sprain it. The ligaments tear and you have to rest the ankle until they repair themselves. If the ankle hurts only for a little while, the ligament has been stretched but not torn.

Gymnasts do exercises that stretch their ligaments so they can move their joints further than most people.

WHAT DO MUSCLES DO?

Muscles are the soft, fleshy parts of the body. They produce the forces you need to move. Particular muscles move particular bones so that you can walk, write, brush your hair, and so on. Muscles in your cheeks pull your face into different positions so that you can frown, smile and talk, for example.

Tendons

Muscles cover your bones. Each muscle is anchored to the bone it covers but is joined to another bone by a **tendon**. This second bone is usually on the other side of a joint. When the muscle pulls the tendon, it moves the other bone at the joint.

Muscles cover the **skeleton** and give your body its rounded shape.

Main muscles

The muscles in your thigh are joined by a tendon to your shin. The tendon pulls the bone to lift and straighten your knee. The muscles that move your thigh lie across your stomach. They are joined by a tendon that stretches over the hip. The muscles in your lower arms move your thumb and fingers. They are joined by very long tendons. You can see them crossing the back of your hand when you stretch your fingers.

Other kinds of muscles

The heart is a special kind of muscle. It pumps blood around the body. A different kind of muscle moves the food you eat through your **intestines**.

The muscles in your thigh move the bones in your lower leg. They are attached by tendons. You can feel two of the tendons at the back of your knee when you lift your leg.

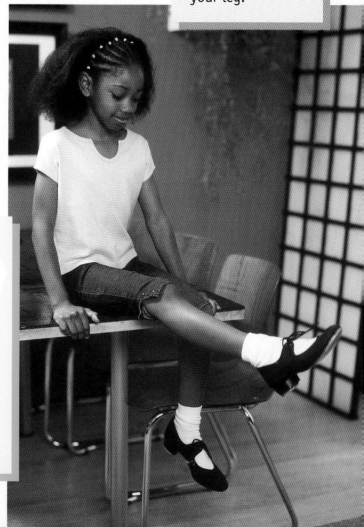

MANY MUSCLES WORK TOGETHER

You have about 650 muscles in your body. Most movements are controlled by several different muscles working together. You use more than 200 different muscles when you walk.

Muscles contract

Muscles produce movement by contracting, that is, by becoming shorter. When a muscle is relaxed, it is soft, but when it is working it becomes stiff and hard. The muscles in your calf move your foot and toes. You can feel them become tight and hard when you move your foot.

Muscles can only pull

Muscles can only contract and pull on a **tendon**. They cannot push. This means that you have one set of muscles to bend your arm and another set to straighten it. The biceps and triceps are both in your upper arm and they work as a pair to bend and straighten the elbow. When the biceps contracts and becomes shorter, it pulls up

The biceps and the triceps work as a pair. The biceps bends the arm and the triceps straightens it.

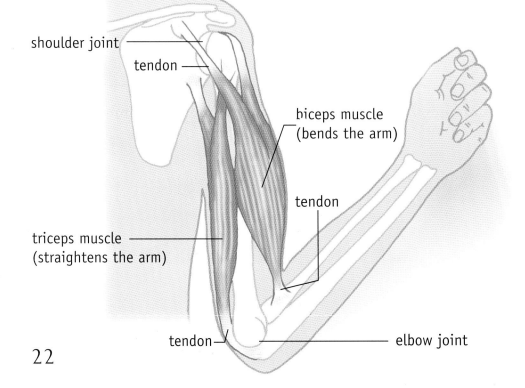

shoulder joint

tendon

biceps muscle (bends the arm)

tendon

triceps muscle (straightens the arm)

tendon

elbow joint

22

the lower arm. At the same time the triceps relaxes. To straighten the arm again the biceps relaxes and returns to its normal length and the triceps contracts.

Pairs of muscles

Almost every movement involves a pair of muscles. Moving your lower jaw up and down to chew, bending and straightening your leg, moving your head from side to side all involve opposing sets of muscles. One set of small muscles shuts your eyelid, another set lifts it open.

Many small muscles work together when you write. It takes a lot of practice for the muscles to make these small, complicated movements smoothly and precisely.

WHICH MUSCLE IS THE LARGEST?

The largest muscle in the human body is the buttock – the muscle you sit on. The strongest muscle is in the jaw and you use it for chewing.

Muscles make up more than a third of the weight of your body. The largest muscle is the muscle in your buttock. Its proper name is *gluteus maximus*. It straightens your hip when you stand up and it gives you a comfortable cushion to sit on. You also use it when you climb up stairs and when you run.

Strongest muscle

The largest muscle, however, is not the strongest muscle. The strongest muscle is the masseter muscle in your jaw that you use to bite. It stretches from the lower jawbone up the side of your face. It clenches your jaw tightly shut.

Muscle fibres

A muscle is made up of bundles of elastic muscle **fibres**. The larger the muscle the more muscle fibres it has. When you eat meat you are eating muscle. You can see the muscle fibres in chicken meat and steak. When you use a muscle only some of the fibres contract and become shorter and thicker. This allows you to make controlled movements. If all the fibres contracted at the same time, you would move in sudden jerks. The more fibres that contract the stronger the muscle reacts.

Inside a muscle fibre

Each muscle fibre is about 40 mm long and is made up of many tiny strands called filaments. In the muscles that move bones, some filaments are thicker and darker than others. They make the fibre look striped.

Muscles are made of bundles of muscle fibres. Each fibre shortens and contracts separately.

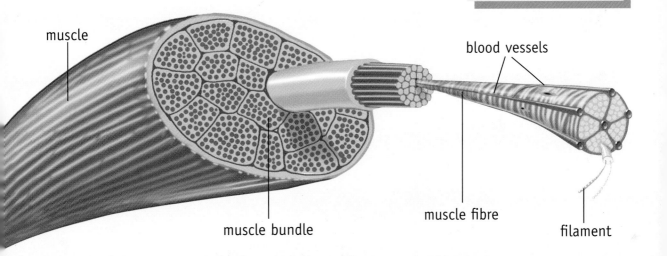

muscle

blood vessels

muscle bundle

muscle fibre

filament

25

Making muscles bigger

Weight-lifters, sprinters and many other athletes have big, bulging muscles. Exercise, such as lifting weights for a short period every day, makes the muscles bigger but it does not increase the number of muscle **fibres**. Instead it increases the number of filaments in each fibre. It also makes the bones and **tendons** stronger. Weight-lifters usually have large chests, shoulders and thighs compared to the rest of their bodies.

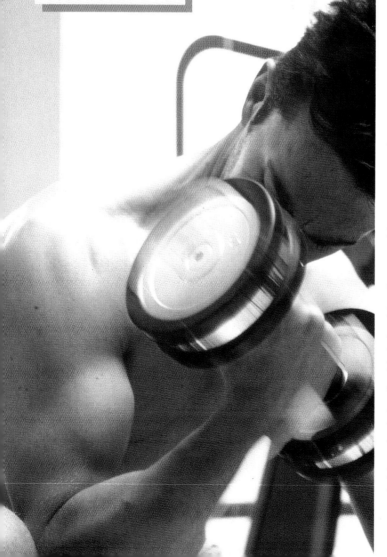

Lifting weights exercises the muscles in the arms, chest, back and thighs. It makes the muscles and bones bigger and stronger.

Making muscles stronger

You can make your muscles stronger without making them bigger. If you take regular exercise every day, such as swimming, cycling or running, your muscle fibres will become better at producing the energy they need to work well. And they can keep working for longer without becoming tired. If you don't use your muscles, however, they become weak.

Cycling strengthens the muscles in your legs, stomach and buttocks. It also makes your heart and lungs work better.

Muscle energy

Muscles use oxygen and glucose (a kind of sugar) to work. Both are brought to them in the blood. The muscle fibres use the oxygen to burn glucose and so release energy to make the muscles work. Everything you do uses energy but some kinds of exercise use more energy than others. Most of the energy is used to make the fibres contract but some of it is changed into heat. This is why exercising also makes you hot.

ENERGY NEEDED FOR DIFFERENT ACTIVITIES

Energy is measured in calories. If you did these activities for an hour, you would use up the amount of energy shown.

running	600 calories/hour
swimming	400 calories/hour
walking	220 calories/hour
reading	80 calories/hour
sleeping	60 calories/hour

WHY DO I GET CRAMP?

You get cramp when some of your muscles contract unexpectedly and do not relax again. Cramp is painful and stops you from using the muscles. People often get cramp in hot weather when they have been sweating a lot. When you sweat your body loses salt as well as water, and the lack of salt causes the cramp.

This girl has cramp in her calf. Pulling her toes towards her will help to make the muscles in her calf relax.

Dealing with cramp

The best way to treat a cramp is to rub or massage the muscle until it gradually relaxes. Keeping the muscle warm also helps. You can avoid getting cramp by stretching your muscles before you exercise, to warm them up, and after exercise, to cool them down. In hot, sweaty weather, drinking plenty of water will help to avoid cramp.

Stomach cramp

One of the most common kinds of cramp is cramp in the muscles of your **intestines**. This gives you a sharp pain in your belly. It is caused by many different things, including food poisoning.

BODY MAP

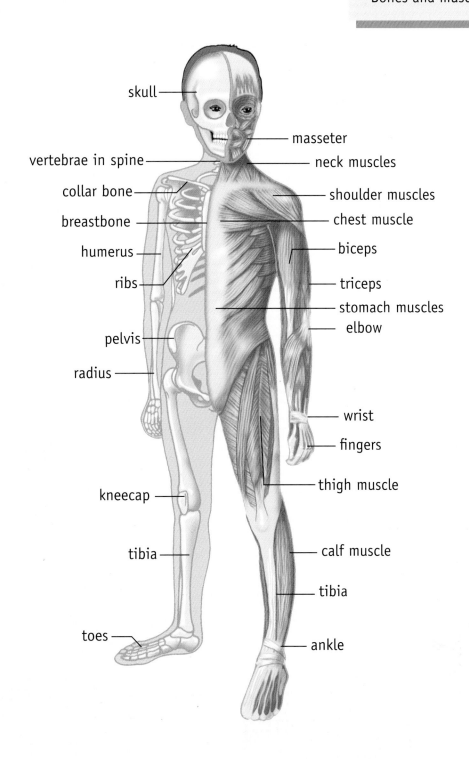

skull

masseter

vertebrae in spine

neck muscles

collar bone

shoulder muscles

breastbone

chest muscle

humerus

biceps

ribs

triceps

stomach muscles

elbow

pelvis

radius

wrist

fingers

thigh muscle

kneecap

tibia

calf muscle

tibia

toes

ankle

GLOSSARY

cartilage   a tough, elastic substance that forms mainly at the end of bones. As bones grow, the cartilage hardens and becomes bone.

cell   the smallest building block of living things. The body has many kinds of cells, including bone cells, muscle cells and blood cells.

fibres   long threads

intestines   the long tube that food passes into after it leaves the stomach

kidneys   organs that clean the blood and produce urine from water and waste chemicals

knuckle   the joints in your fingers and thumb

marrow   the soft, jelly-like substance found at the centre of many bones

minerals   chemicals that are usually found in rocks and soil. The body needs several minerals, which it gets from the food you eat.

nerves   pathways that carry messages from the brain to the muscles and from the senses to the brain

organ   part of the body that carries out a particular process. The stomach, heart and kidneys are all organs.

puberty   the time (usually between ages ten and sixteen) during which a child's body changes so that he or she is able to produce children

skeleton   the body's frame, which is made up of bones

tendon   a tough band that joins a muscle to a bone

vertebrae   the bones of the spine

vertebra   one of the vertebrae

FURTHER READING

Body Books: Get a move on! A Ganeri, 2002, Evans Books

Body matters: Why do I vomit? and other questions about digestion, A Royston, 2002, Heinemann Library

Body matters: Why do I get toothache? and other questions about nerves, A Royston, 2002, Heinemann Library

Look at your body: Skeleton, S Parker, 2001, Franklin Watts

INDEX

Titles in the *Body Matters* series include:

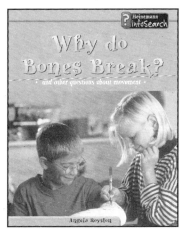

Hardback   0431 11075 1

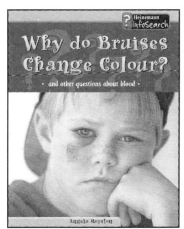

Hardback   0431 11073 5

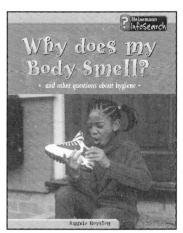

Hardback   0431 11077 8

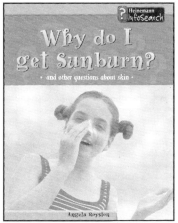

Hardback   0431 11078 6

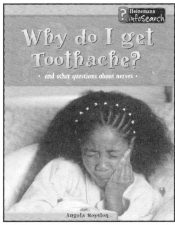

Hardback   0431 11076 X

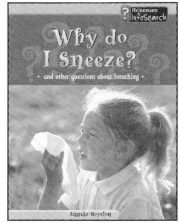

Hardback   0431 11070 0

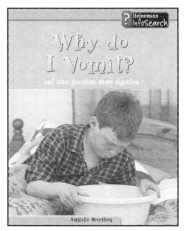

Hardback   0431 11072 7

Hardback   0431 11071 9

Find out about the other titles in this series on our website www.heinemann.co.uk/library